APPLEFORD
a Berkshire village

Vera Reynolds

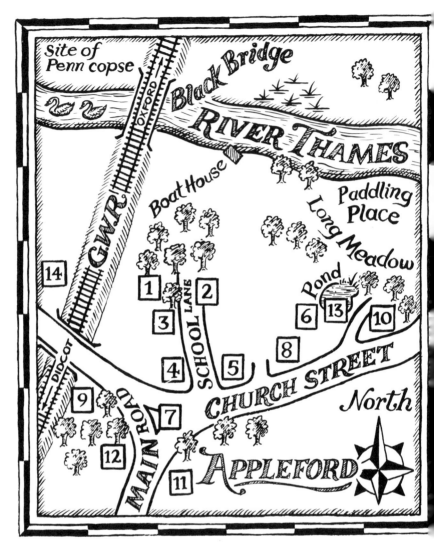

1. Barnards
2. Barnards' Chapel
3. Site of School
4. Orchard House
5. The Grove
6. Manor Farm
7. Site of Knapp Tree
8. Old Thatch
9. Appleford Halt
10. Church of St.Peter and St.Paul
11. The Carpenters Arms
12. Site of The Black Horse
13. Site of Benedictine Monks' Fishery

APPLEFORD
a Berkshire village

Vera Reynolds

BARNWORKS
publishing

PULBOROUGH, ENGLAND

First published in 1996 in Great Britain by
Barnworks Publishing
Bury, Pulborough,
West Sussex RH20 1PA

British Library Cataloguing in Publication Data.
A catalogue record for this book is available from the British Library.

Paperback edition: ISBN: 1-899174-03-6

Printed and bound by Redwood Press, Trowbridge, Wiltshire

Cover design and illustrations by Simon Abbott

CONTENTS

Acknowledgements

Foreword

The Village of Appleford	1
Orchard House	8
The School	10
Long Meadow	17
Old Thatch	20
The Church of St Peter and St Paul	28
Manor Farm	33
Barnards	38
The Post Office	41
The Village Pubs	44
Changing Times	48
APPLEFORD Recipes	52

For my dear grandchildren

ACKNOWLEDGEMENTS

I have received help and encouragement from many people without whom this little book would not have been possible.

My thanks go to the staff of the Reading Record Office and Abingdon Library. To my friends for telling me their memories, particularly Ron Meadham, Doreen Hartwright and the late Mrs Adeline Stunell. Also to Mr A. Brown of Morlands plc, who helped with my research into the village public houses.

I am very grateful to Professor Paul Foster of the Chichester Institute for Higher Education at Bishop Otter College for encouraging me to write my memories, to Sally Mills and Anna Kemble who read the manuscript and Nicky Belcher for typing it.

Wartime harvesting.

FOREWORD

As the present owner of Barnards I was asked by the author to assist with her monograph of Appleford.

In her youth Barnards was known as 'the big house' and in its grounds stood a fifteenth century chapel.

Discussing the old days, we realise now what an important part the chapel played in the life of the village. Some of the less obvious activities that took place in this versatile building were whist drives, dances, wedding receptions, cricket team teas, refreshments for shooting parties, billiards and, once during the Second World War, it served as a temporary mortuary for drowned paratroopers. In other words it was a focal point for the village which did not have a village hall in those days.

I am sorry to have to say that the chapel no longer exists, having been demolished in 1966.

The Parachute Exercise mentioned in the chapter on Old Thatch took place in late May and early June 1944, just before D-Day. The rumour that it was a rehearsal for Arnhem has been discounted as only seven days notice was given for operation 'Market Garden' in September 1944.

This little book presents a delightful, nostalgic picture of a rural village in the 'good old days' before power stations, gravel pits and rubbish dumps. A village of charm and thatched cottages with twice as many pubs as at present.

We can imagine the village schoolchildren, including the author when young, dancing round the maypole on Barnards' lawns.

From our house it is still possible to see the church with its arrow-piercing spire in spite of much new building which has taken place in recent years. A church where our eldest son was married and our four grandchildren christened.

I hope, therefore, that those who read this book will feel part of Appleford, even if it is no longer Appleford, Berkshire.

Major W.F.C. Robertson, DWR (Ret'd.)
May 1996

Barnards - detail from a sketch by Ken Messer.

The Village of Appleford

The Abbey (Abingdon Abbey) holds Apleford (Appleford) in demesne. T.R.E* as now it was assessed at 5 hides. There is land for six and a half ploughs. On the demesne are 2 and (there are) 14 villians and 20 borders with 4 ploughs. One serf is there and 2 mills worth (de) 25 shillings and a fishery worth (de) 10 shillings and 60 acres of meadow, and 21 shillings of profits (de ducia) from the demesne land. Of this land Robert holds 1 hide and he has two borders there. The whole was worth T.R.E. 9 pounds; and afterwards, as now, the same.

Domesday Book Berkshire entry 1924 edition

A border was one who dwelt on land where he was born, demesne means manor lands, a villian was a free villager while a serf was a labourer bound to and transferred with the land.

Appleford is a small, sleepy village nestling on the banks of the River Thames in Oxfordshire between its neighbouring market towns of Abingdon and Wallingford. It is certainly not a striking place. If you were not a visitor or resident you would drive straight through on the B1406 to Abingdon and Wallingford scarcely glancing at the council houses, a few modern bungalows and the flat agricultural land. When I see the level-crossing gates and the signal box where my father used to work, I know I am home. Past the garage that used to be Mr Jennings' Blacksmith's

---

* T.R.E. tempore regis Edwardi - in King Edward's time
   i.e. before 1066

Forge, the council houses where several of my school friends used to live and turn right past Knapp Tree and you are in Church Street. Immediately one can see the grey thatched roof of the old cottage where I lived in the 1930s and 1940s. To many of us who grew up in the village and left because our careers, lives and fortunes have taken us away from its peace and tranquillity, Appleford is still home.

Home goes back a long way. In the monograph 'Edward Bradstock of Appleford' by Edward J. King details are given of a Romano-British settlement that was discovered by Arthur Napper, the owner of Bridge Farm in 1954. He dug up a hoard of several thousand Roman coins with his tractor. These coins, which were in two earthenware pots, had lain there for 1,600 years. Most of them were of the period 320—350 A.D. at a time when inflation was rife in the decaying Roman Empire. We shall never know whether they were the property of a farmer or trader. The growing crops on the flat fields still show faint lines, rectangles and circles, which centuries of cultivation have failed to erase. The markings are thought to be traces of British settlements and remains of Romano-British buildings.

In the Berkshire Archaeological Journal 1-2 1939, an item on Berkshire barrows notes that:

> *There are at least four circles between Appleford*
> *and Moor Ditch, revealed on air-photographs.*
> *Sites visited 26.2.39. nothing visible.*

The next evidence of Appleford's history can be traced to Anglo-Saxon times, when the village received its name in a charter granted by King Alfred (871-901). It was then a hamlet. The name Appleford was originally spelt with one 'p' and it was not until the eighteenth century that it was spelt with two 'p's on a regular basis. The name is thought to be derived from the ford across the River Thames which was used to transport the fruit grown in the orchards at Hagbourne and Harwell in Berkshire to the markets in Oxfordshire. The infamous highwayman Dick Turpin allegedly made the Manor Farm in Church Street into his headquarters. This farm is only a few minutes' ride from the river. When Dick Turpin had been 'working' the London-Oxford Road, the ford offered easy access for himself and his booty from the Oxfordshire side of the river to his hideaway in the farm in Berkshire. Appleford was one of the few places south of Oxford where the river could be crossed on foot.

Appleford's school children in the 1930s and 1940s learned to swim in the Thames where the ford was reputed to have existed. There was a small inlet along the bank of the river and we called it the 'paddling place'. I remember we were allowed to swim out as far as an old tree stump, which we always believed to be the root of an apple tree. It was certainly very shallow there, and you could walk out about a third of the way across the river. The bed of the river was then much deeper as it was regularly used by passing pleasure steamers and motor launches. When we had learned to swim we were allowed to progress to 'the big place', a few yards along the bank to the west of the inlet, the water was much deeper there. I am not sure who made that rule.

I now know that this was all in our imagination and our paddling place was not the site of the ford. Talking to Major Robertson, the present owner of Barnards in the autumn of 1994, he assured me that the ford was at the end of a field which was originally Barnards' land. When I chatted to Mrs Adeline Stunell who lived in Appleford for many years, she almost convinced me that the ford was in the backwater by the Weir at the far end of Long Meadow. It is feasible that there was a ford there, one bank of this narrow backwater is in Appleford, but the opposite side is in Long Wittenham. That could well have been a ford but not Dick Turpin's escape route from Oxfordshire. My friend Ron Meadham agrees with Mrs Stunell who told me, "I know it's there — I've walked across it". He told me recently that in his youth he tried to walk across the backwater and found that by zig-zagging across the water you could walk from Long Meadow to Long Wittenham. The most likely place for the ford used by Dick

Turpin is at the end of Barnards near the railway bridge and only two fields gallop from Manor Farm.

When I took my children to the paddling place in the 1960s, they loved it. They had learned to swim in the hot and steamy atmosphere of an indoor swimming pool and had no idea you could actually swim in a river. We had taken a picnic, as my mother had done some thirty years earlier. Sitting on the river bank in the warm sunshine with the birds singing and the butterflies hovering around was a new experience for two city-born small boys. Long Meadow was a kaleidoscope of colours — yellow buttercups and white moon daisies, reminding me of the days when, as a child, I swam there with my friends and we picked bunches of wild flowers to take home to our mothers.

The village, like so many agricultural communities in 1066, consisted of two streets. The Main Road (now the B1406) and Church Street. From Church Street a turning to the left leads you into School Lane, with Orchard House on the corner. Further down you find Old Thatch on your left, then Manor Farm. At the end of the village stands the church of St. Peter and St. Paul. The entire village, until the building of the embankments for the Great Western Railway in 1840, was surrounded by flat farm land. The whole overlooked to the east by the Sinodon Hills at Long Wittenham — known to us as Wittenham Clumps.

> *APPLEFORD, Apleford, XI Cent. Apulford XVI Cent. was evidently part of the royal demesne when King Alfred sold its 5 hides to his faithful Deormod for 50 mancuses of gold. From Deormod and his heim* it must have passed to Abingdon Abbey which held it in demesne in 1086, when it was assessed, as before the Conquest, at 5 hides, the Abbey continued to hold the manor until the dissolution of the monasteries.*
> * heir

The Victorian County History of Berkshire 1924 confirms that:
> *'Robert held 1 hide of the Abbey 1086', and suggests that perhaps the hide was restored after many disputes with Abingdon Abbey by Henry II. Shortly after this 'Abbot Walchelin granted it in fee to Pain de Appleford for an annual payment of 20s. By a charter of Henry II in 1288 the Abbey claimed free warren here, as in all demesnes'.*

Records kept by unnamed monks in the Abbey give us glimpses of life at the Manor and farms. Much of the rent for the farms was paid in food-stuffs. The Abbot receiving 'sticks' of eels (a stick with the branches chopped short -the gill of the eel would be hooked on to the branch) from the Appleford fisheries. One fishery was in the farmyard of Manor Farm, close to the church, and the other on the land where The Carpenters Arms public house now stands.

The Abbey withstood several disasters. In 1327 it was sacked by a mob, when priceless documents were destroyed. In 1349 the Black Death swept the country. How these crises affected the simple village people, tilling their soil and paying their dues in labour, or fruit from their labours, is not recorded. Neither do we know how they were treated by their masters, the Benedictine monks. One thing is certain, no-one in Appleford would ever have contemplated the sudden disappearance of the Abbey, and with it their masters. What a complete change to their way of living must have swept through the villages, when in 1538 a long chapter of Appleford's history came to an end. During the reign of Henry VIII Abingdon Abbey was one of the first great religious houses to surrender. The Abbot was allowed to retire and the monks were dispersed. Suddenly, the Great Abbey was gone. Ruins of the building can still be seen in the Abbey grounds in Abingdon. These buildings were plundered and despoiled. Its money and lands, together with its rich endowments, passed into the hands of the Crown.

Agriculture was the principal, if not the only, industry in those early days. Apart from the fish ponds where fish were raised for the monks, there was a mill to which farmers around brought their corn to be ground.

According to The Berkshire Book published by Berkshire Federation of Women's Institutes in 1939 a few fields had names, for some of which no reason can now be given. Gooseacre is an exception, the name obviously indicating its former use. Other names are Pottles, Codmore (or Cotmoor), this land lies just under a quarter of a mile south of Hill Farm, Sand Furlong, Badcock's, Moorpiece, Horstleys or Horseleys, the Common, and the Moors or Moor Meadow. The latter is the field immediately north of Easton's plantation, the woodland at the south end of the parish. Other field names include Coedreys, Gravel Piece and New Pump Piece. A 'piece' according to Wright's 'Dialect Dictionary' is

> *'an indefinite space or distance'; whence it may be inferred that the areas so named were not clearly defined.*

I am unable to say where all these fields were in the village. I do remember the Grove, a small piece of land which belonged to Manor Farm, in Church Street. Long Meadow is also Manor Farm land which runs from our paddling place to the Appleford Weir; its only boundaries were the River Thames on one side and a hedge with a footpath running alongside, on the other. We called this footpath Meadow Hedge. In my childhood you could cross the meadow at Oak Style and walk a footpath to Stream Ditch which then ran into a backwater, leading to the Weir. This narrow ditch separates the villages of Long Wittenham and Appleford.

It is extraordinary how Manor Farm, Orchard House, Barnards and Old Thatch have survived since the days of Charles II. The properties in Church Street would have seen the fighting on Manor Farm land in the seventeenth century, when Appleford was strictly Puritan and fought the Royalist Cavalry. Evidence of the fighting was discovered on this land when men, levelling mounds to make a track for agricultural machinery, found a number of skeletons buried a few feet below the surface.

The Industrial Revolution would have had a tremendous effect on the men and their families who were working on the land. The altered industrial conditions tempted large numbers of small farmers and peasants from their holdings. Towards the end of the nineteenth century farmers suffered serious setbacks when agriculture collapsed in the face of pressure from foreign competition. It was in the twentieth century, during the Second World War, that farming and the farmers' lot improved. Farmers, and their workers, were a vital part of the war effort. Their expertise was needed to produce corn and vegetables to help feed the nation. Now in 1996 this tiny part of England, so steeped in history, can no longer follow its own agricultural policy; the majority of its laws are passed by the European Economic Community in Brussels.

From the rule of the Benedictine monks to the laws of the EEC.

What a glorious pageant of history these properties have witnessed and I feel some of their stories should be told...

Orchard House
formerly The Old Parsonage

This house still contains portions of the sixteenth century building of Bradstock's day, and its title-deeds identify it as part of the properties conveyed to him by Anthony Weekes, or Mason, by an Indenture of the 'twenty-fifth year of the reign of Queen Elizabeth and enrolled in the Court of Exchequer in the fifteenth year of the reign of King Charles the First'.

Edmund Bradstock of Appleford
Edward J. King

The original Indenture and Will of Edward Bradstock can be seen in the Record Office in Shire Hall, Reading.

This large rambling house still stands on the corner of School Lane, in the remains of its once large garden and orchards surrounded by a high stone wall. Like Barnards it was one house with subsequent additions of periods ranging from Elizabethan to Victorian.

The drawing room is possibly late Elizabethan or early Stuart. It contains a fireplace of the same era with herringbone brickwork in the chimney place. At least one interior wall is wattle and daub.

On the outside you can see one window that has been bricked up (a memorial of Pitt's Window Tax) and several arches which suggest doors that have also been bricked in. The roof is probably Georgian. Part of the orchard can still be seen on the western side of the house, but much of the garden has been taken for building first the school and later the houses in School Lane.

All evidence indicates that when Edmund Bradstock married Jane Justice in 1579 they made their home in the house which was formerly called The Old Parsonage. Its title-deeds identify it as part of the properties conveyed to him by Anthony Weekes, who took the name Mason.

We do not know whether he gave the land for the school to be built on during his lifetime or if this was done by his executor after his wife's death. But it is certain that the land for the school buildings and playground were cut from the garden and orchard of the homestead.

When we were children running down School Lane, we would pass Orchard House on the corner and run alongside the high stone wall. It was impossible for us to see into the garden or the orchard. Only very occasionally did we see the owners, a Mr and Mrs Cummins. Mrs Doreen Hartwright of Hartwright House remembers the Cummins as 'real old English gentry'. Mrs Cummins had a cat which produced kittens twice a year. Everyone dreaded seeing Mrs Cummins coming towards their house because one nearly always ended up with an unwanted kitten. We were always in awe of the people that lived behind the high walls. When we reached the end of the wall we would turn left into our playground.

The School

...to the whole and only intent use and purpose
as they and every one of them shall and must
undoubtedly answer to Almighty God for the
contrary at the dreadful Day of Judgement, that
they shall appoint, nominate, chose and place a
Godly learned and sufficient school master to
teach in true religion and learning always twenty
scholars of the poor inhabitants sons of Sutton
Courtenay and Appleford

Edmund Bradstock of Appleford.

Edward J. King

It was a provision of Edmund Bradstock's Will that he left 'the messuage and three yard lands' strictly to provide a school for the poor children of the village. He left this to his wife, provided she remained unmarried. Should she remarry the house and land were to be placed in the care of his nephews, Edmund Bradstock, the younger, to Thomas Justice of Sutton Courtenay and to Edmund Ridar of Abingdon, in succession. This cautious provision was to stop the 'messuage and three yard lands' from falling into the hands of an unscrupulous second husband, who might ignore his wish - the endowment of his school.

The Victorian County History of Berkshire (1924) confirms that:

A free school was launched in 1607 for thirteen
children from Sutton Courtenay and seven from
Appleford. The tiny village school was enlarged
in 1896. Apart from the names of the
schoolmasters, little is known of its early days.
Mr Devoroux Bollinger, Vicar of North Molton
and schoolmaster of Appleford died in 1689. The
burials of Thomas Lawrence, Bachelor of Arts

> *(1733) and of Edward Blandy (1761) are recorded in the Register.*

We do know that in 1875 the Appleford schoolmaster was taking girls as well as boys, and this is thought to be inconsistent with Edmund Bradstock's Will.

> *The Charity Commissioners' Report of 1908 brings the history of Edmund Bradstock's Trusts to the beginning of the present century. The Report mentions that under a scheme approved by the Court of Chancery in 1860 a body of seven Trustees (to include the Vicar of Sutton Courtenay, if willing to act - he would also have been the Vicar of Appleford - as the two parishes shared a Vicar) was set up to administer the school charity.*

> Edmund Bradstock of Appleford
> Edward J. King

It was the sole task of this body to administer the income from the Trust to maintain the school and its playground and to appoint a master who would be a member of the Church of England. He would then be able to take girls in the school as well as the free boys. The children must be taught religion in accordance with the beliefs of the Anglican church, but consideration had always to be given to the religious scruples of parents that were members of other denominations.

The list of subjects to be taught is ambitious and would probably have been more appropriate to a grammar school, such as reading, arithmetic, geography, history, mathematics, natural philosophy, land-surveying drawing, designing, Latin, general English literature and composition. When I attended the school in the 1930s we were taught reading, writing, geography, history, spelling, mathematics, drawing, English literature, composition, poetry, music, needlework and P.E and games. Edmund Bradstock's wishes and dreams had materialised and it was due to his generosity that we had an extremely good church school in the village. We children received a thorough education with strict discipline.

We did have playtimes, when boys and girls could all play together and would often play games like 'Here we come gathering nuts in May...'

Another game we often played was where we all formed a ring with one child standing outside; we sang 'In and out the windows...'

The oldest existing Log Book of the school opens on the 3rd April 1876, with the words 'Appleford School opened this day. J. H. Woolford commenced my duties as a teacher'. The Inspector's Report that year states: 'The School has just re-opened but it is promising'.

I have been unable to trace when the school was closed, nor any indication of the duration of its closure.

When the school was re-opened, the previously anonymous pupils became named. The first entry in the school records of April 1882, tells us that David Brown received the annual Bishop's Prize for scripture. From then on the Log Book listed other prize-winners, absentees and 'sinners'. Records show the Bishop's Prize was awarded in 1888 to Alice Townsend, to Edith Gate in 1894, and to Ernest Collett in 1901. Others listed as Bishop's Prize winners were Henry Clifford, Lily Reynolds (my aunt) and Joseph Brown, who was a close friend of my father.

The list of School Managers includes Mr Edward Pullen, then farmer of Manor Farm and Miss Tolson, who lived in the Wooden House in Church Street with Miss Jenkins. I can just remember Miss Letitia Jenkins, a tiny lady, playing the organ in church every Sunday. Teachers listed included Mr Baldwin, Mrs Hedges and Mrs Hillsdon. Mrs Hillsdon and Mrs Skinner were teaching at the school when I and my friends attended in 1934 - until we left for schools in Didcot in 1940. Mrs Hillsdon remained at the school until 1953, when she had completed a quarter of a century of teaching. She was succeeded by Miss

Helen Williams, who remained there until the school was closed in 1961.

The oldest resident of Appleford I traced, was Mrs Adeline Stunell, who attended the school in 1918. At that time Mrs Baldwin was headmistress and Miss Chesterman taught the infants. Mrs Stunell remembered the teachers and pupils celebrated the end of World War I by marching round the Knapp Tree, saluting the flag and singing 'Land of Hope and Glory'.

On recalling her nine years at school, Mrs Stunell remembered five governesses during that period, who all lived in School House. She told me, "We always wore knitted dresses, which our Mam made for us. A lot of the girls wore white starched overalls to keep their clothes clean, we didn't – our Mam didn't make us. We did not pay to go to school like they did in Abingdon". Mrs Stunell left school at the age of fourteen in 1927.

In the days between the wars whist drives and dances, which we called 'sixpenny hops', were held in the school. The larger classroom was also used for cricket teas.

Mrs Mary Hillsdon was appointed Head Mistress at Appleford School on 9th August 1929. She was paid the sum of £252.10s per annum. In an agreement between Mrs Hillsdon and Miss Gladys Maud Tolson, a school governor, the Hillsdon family were allowed to rent School House for £9.00 a year. During my school days Mr and Mrs Hillsdon lived in the bungalow almost opposite Old Thatch. School House was rented to Mr and Mrs Joe Brown and their children Danny and Betty. Mr Brown was then the school caretaker and his wife, the church cleaner.

Mrs Dorothy Skinner of Sutton Courtenay was appointed Infant teacher on 28th June 1935.

During 1935, several improvements were made to the school. On 19th February 1935 J.Chambers, Builder of Sutton Courtenay quoted:

re:	*Ceiling in Schoolroom*	*£15.10.0*
	Distemper White	*£12.18.6*
	Replace Window	*£ 7.15.0*

In 1936, Stone and Duke, Electrical Contractor of Oxford quoted:

> *To install Electricity*
> *To the School* £8.0.0
> *To the School House* £4.2.6
> *Both to be guaranteed for twenty-four calendar months.*

A School Inspector reported on 10th May 1939 that:

> *The upper group here is rather an awkward one, owing to its wide age range, and the children vary a good deal in ability. The boys, (junior only) are active and responsive, but the girls are generally a shade diffident. Writing and English are good subjects. Essential subjects are quite successful.*

A further report dated 5th November, 1940 states:

> *A second visit fully confirms the good impression I formed of the school. What might be termed its general atmosphere is particularly good.*

The report went on to say that:

> *The Headmistress has a list of everything that is required. Children would much appreciate copies of 'The Children's Worship', cost 6d and 'A Child's Guide to Morning Prayer' again only 6d. I can assure the managers that it is well worth while spending money on a school like this.*

When my friend Ron came to visit me in Sussex during the summer of 1995 I said to him, "I want to pick your brains about Appleford School, Ron".

"That's a tall order, Vera, it's a long time ago we went to school", he replied. He went on to say, "I do remember the furniture, the little desks and Mrs Hillsdon's tall desk which stood by that old coke stove and those awful little bottles of milk warming on top. I hated that milk". Those little bottles of milk are one of my strongest memories. I too hated these and always tried to get my friend Ethel to drink mine.

"Do you remember what you wore?", I asked him next.

"Yes," he replied, "I do – grey pullovers, white shirts, navy blue trousers, grey socks and black plimsolls, our mother couldn't afford to buy us shoes". (Ron was one of a large family).

"What about the maypole, did the boys join in the maypole dancing, because if you remember we used to take the maypole to Barnards, when Mrs and Mrs Menteath lived there, to dance on the lawn. I've still got my Silver Jubilee* mug that we were given there," I said.

"Yes, we had to dance and some of us were in the choir. Old Mr Powell, you remember him, lived down by the church, he kept us lads in order. Appleford had a good choir then".

In 1945 Mrs Stuart-Menteath of Barnards became a school governor and was responsible for several improvements that were made to the school, including a tarmac playground. She also asked Shire Hall at Reading to increase the wages of the school cleaner when Mrs Green resigned. This was agreed and on 13th August 1945 the wages were increased to £2 per month during the summer and £3 a month in the winter. It was Mrs Stuart-Menteath who suggested that the older children should go to school in Didcot. This idea was put to the Education Department in Shire Hall. It was in 1940, when we were eleven years of age, that we went to the Secondary Modern School in Didcot; boys and girls going to separate schools. There was no school bus for us to use. The Education Department supplied bicycles for those children who did not have their own. Those of us that were fortunate enough to have our own bikes were paid one penny a day for the maintenance of our machines.

Being a Church of England school we were expected to attend church regularly. All the school would go to church on Feast

---

*   To commemorate the Silver Jubilee of King George V
    and Queen Mary's accession to the throne (1910–1935)

Days, such as Ascension Day. In the early years of the school the children would 'goe the perambulation on Ascension Day' [beating the bounds]. We would walk down School Lane and Church Street in a crocodile line. After church we knew that we were free for the rest of the day — no more school.

I asked Mrs Stunell if she went to church on Ascension Day.

"Of course we did, and we did not get the day off after church, like you. We had to go back to school".

While Mrs Stunell was reminiscing about her schooldays, she said,

"Don't forget John Faulkner, the jockey. If I remember he had thirty-two children all of whom went to Appleford School - but he did have two wives".

Then I discovered that his son, Jimmy had thirty-three children by three wives. Mrs Stunell continued,

"Billy and Daphne Faulkner went to school with you, they lived in the cottages opposite your grandparents' in Main Road".

My grandparents lived in Rose Cottage.

John Faulkner began his career as an apprentice to Isaac Walcol, who trained on Salisbury Plain. By 1851 he was in regular employment as a jockey at the weight of 4st 7lbs or 28.5 kilos. Both he and his son, Jimmy, were celebrated jockeys. John was in his one hundred and fifth year when he died in 1933. John is buried in the churchyard. Jimmy was ninety-seven years old when he died in Barnes in Surrey. The fame of these two men does not rest on their longevity or on the size of their families – amazing as they were. Each man in his time became the oldest jockey in England - giving Appleford distinction in the racing world. John Faulkner's first winner, ridden at Epsom while he was still a stable-lad, earned him the payment of threepence. He rode in his first Derby in 1860. He was seventy-four years old when he rode in his last race, a steeple-chase at Abingdon. There are no members of the Faulkner family living in Appleford at the time of writing.

Long Meadow

Elderberry wine was made by at least one housewife until a very short time since. Mr Tame states that many people drank this beverage to excess. Cowslip wine was also made at one time but this vintage has gone out of use latterly.

The Berkshire Book
Berkshire Federation of W.I's. 1939

Appleford was essentially cowslip country. The meadow was always a profusion of colour in the spring and summer. They grew in abundance in Long Meadow. In my adult years, I thought we were the original vandals that, by picking too many cowslips (*Primula Veris*), we caused the flowers to become an endangered species. Now I know the reason is the excessive use of chemicals on the fields.

Long Meadow on a bright, sunny spring morning was paradise to us children. We were free after the Ascension Day Service. Free to go and swim in the paddling place and play in the meadow. Our mothers would come with picnic baskets and idle the hours away chatting on the river banks. One or the other would occasionally call,

"Don't go out too far".

When we tired of swimming we played tag, hide 'n seek, rounders and run in the meadow, picking armfuls of wild flowers to take home. Cowslips were a favourite flower, but the humble buttercup (*Ranunculus Bulbous*) was there too - shining yellow petals, soft like satin. We would run all the way down to Oak Style - a stile beside an oak tree to enable walkers to cross from Meadow Hedge to the footpath to Stream Ditch. In the marshy ground by the stile, we would find the delicate mauve cuckoo flowers (*Cardaniemo Fraternis*). If we were very quiet and really lucky, we might see a brilliantly coloured kingfisher flying along the ditch. Simple pleasures.

In winter the marshy ground at Oak Style flooded. On frosty nights the floodwater would freeze. I remember on bright moonlight evenings being taken by my father to skate and slide on the ice. Can you imagine the joy, freedom and exhilaration of sliding on the ice on a cold and frosty evening under a full moon? My grandfather told the story of the extremely hard winter in 1871 when Farmer Pullen roasted an ox on the Thames, and the whole village enjoyed a party on the ice.

My grandfather spent many hours in his retirement walking in Long Meadow – especially in the spring. He was quite sure that he could forecast the weather by looking at the developing buds on the trees and the habits of the wildlife. Some of his favourite sayings were:

> If the ash before the oak,
> We will get a darn good soak,
> If the oak before the ash
> We will only get a splash.

> No weather is ill,
> If the wind be still,
> But rough wind and storm,
> Works plenty of harm.

> If it rains on Easter Day,
> Plenty of grass but not much hay.

The river bank was very popular with fishermen. Every weekend during the fishing season, they would come to Appleford from London, to fish for roach and perch in the river. Many of them stayed for a week's fishing holiday in the farm cottages. Mother had fishermen to stay regularly at Old Thatch. These London men brought a little prosperity to the village. They would pay to stay in the cottages and pass the evenings away enjoying a pint of local beer in The Carpenters Arms, or The Black Horse public houses. They also created work for the Water Bailiff. In my memory Mr Taylor, who was also the landlord of The Carpenters Arms, was employed by the Thames Conservancy throughout the fishing season to collect fees from the fishermen. His stretch of water was from the Railway Bridge to the weir.

Farmer Pullen's cows would graze peacefully in Long Meadow. They were not interrupted by us children or the fishermen. Indeed Long Meadow through each season of the year, gave pleasure to many people.

I can remember days when families would arrive at Appleford Halt by train from Didcot, armed with picnics and swimming costumes to spend a day by the river. The children would swim in the paddling place and, like us village children, would go home with bunches of wild flowers.

Old Thatch

Recently, Mr and Mrs Robinson of Appleford were making alterations to the kitchen of their 17th century timber framed cottage when they found, embedded in the heavy clay floor 2-3" below the surface, two broken cooking pots... Beneath the doorway in the centre of the partition was found a late 15th century Nuremberg token... Mrs Degous, an expert on medieval and post-medieval pottery, examined the pots and she says they are probably 17th century or early 18th century.

Report by Christine Bloxham
Oxfordshire County Museum July, 1978

This suggests that the cottage has been facing the Sinodun Hills since the reign of Charles II. When I lived there in the 1930s and 1940s our only lighting for most of that period was by a paraffin lamp and candles. There was no mains water. All our water was drawn from the well, which was outside, opposite a copper – this large vessel was used for boiling clothes. It was heated by a very small coal fire below. The only heating indoors was an open fire in the living room. My father, because he worked for the Railway Company, was able to buy a ton of coal once a year from them, for which he paid £1. He was able to buy a truck load of used railway sleepers to chop for firewood for £1. (I now pay £8 cwt for my coal). Our toilet was a wooden outhouse in the garden. Weekly baths were taken in a huge tin bath in front of the fire. I do remember how cold it was in the bedrooms in the winter months.

In the autumn we used to sit in the lamplight making coloured rings and sticking them together to form paper chains. The Christmas Puddings[*] bubbled in their saucepans on the fire.

Mother made the puddings in October when we always had a stir and a wish. There was a pudding for Granny Reynolds in Rose Cottage, my granny in Haddenham, Buckinghamshire and one to be put by for Easter Day. This cottage had been my home for over twenty years. It was then one of two farm cottages, part of the Manor Farm estate owned by Squire Eyston of East Hendred. The smaller cottage, one bedroom and one living room was occupied by Mrs Barrett, who was employed as housekeeper to Farmer Pullen. When Mrs Barrett died, my father paid an additional sixpence a week to rent the two extra rooms, he was then paying ten shillings and sixpence a week to rent our home.

I had no idea how we came to live there as my father was a Great Western Railway signalman and my grandfather, Willie Reynolds, was a Great Western Railway ganger. We had no connections with the farm. However, Mrs Stunell said, "The house was previously occupied by old Joby Carter, who worked for Mr Pullen. He was the road sweeper for Church Street only.
The street belonged to Manor Farm, from Knapp Tree to the church and it was his job to sweep it every Saturday, and all the farmyard and the church path for the ladies to walk to the church on Sunday morning. Your granny always wore a long black skirt to church. He fell down and died and Mr Pullen decided not to employ another road-sweeper – that's how your father got the cottage".

During Mr Carter's time of residence there was a row of three cottages opposite Old Thatch. These cottages were demolished when the council houses in Main Road were built. A bungalow was built on this plot by Mr and Mrs Harry Clifford. He worked in the Great Western Railway Provender Stores in Didcot. They lived in the bungalow with their four daughters, Phyllis, Adeline

---

[*] Appleford Christmas Pudding - see recipe at end of book.

(Mrs Stunell), Florence and Dorothy. Mrs Clifford was known in the village as 'Lady Clifford', because she wore bright blue stockings and was one of the first people to own a bicycle.

The old house has weathered many storms and its occupants would most certainly have been affected by the agricultural depression in 1874, the wars of this century, and the abdication of Edward VIII. My father told me that the Prince of Wales would ride across Manor Farm fields with the Oxford College Beagles. Mr Johnny Meadham says he remembers the Prince stopping to talk to the beaters in the shooting season. The farm workers would act as beaters, one who rouses or beats up game, to the shoot and I understand they had a great respect for the Prince of Wales.

In July 1992 Mr and Mrs Robinson, who now own the cottage, kindly invited me to visit their home. It had been completely renovated but I was able to tell them a little of what the cottage was like in the 1930s.

"The stairs were where your kitchen is, the open fire on that wall, with a cupboard either side, the large cupboard on the right of the fireplace was used as our airing cupboard, with a bread oven to the left".

The big oak beams can still be seen in the living room and I could picture how they used to be adorned with holly and home-made paper chains. A hall now joins the two cottages together. The hall is where the copper stood outside, opposite the well. When we lived in Old Thatch, during the warm summer months, mother always kept the milk and butter in a bucket in the well to keep it cold. I was staggered by the improvements that had been made to the cottage. It now had a new look. I was in no way distressed by the changes, my thoughts were to wonder how mother coped? Of course, many others lived in similar cottages without the modern conveniences we take for granted today. When I remember it took all day Monday to do the washing, filling the copper with water from the well, boiling the water, then the washing would be boiled. It was quite a task. I now realise

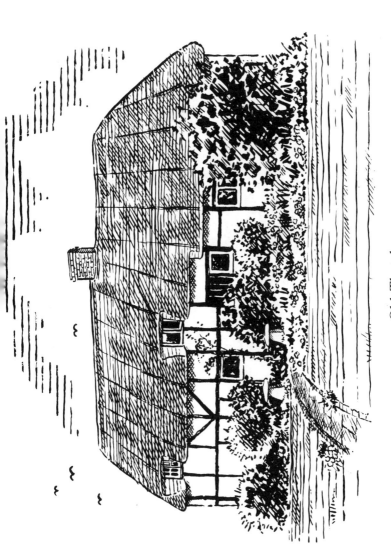

Old Thatch.

The School.

how hard mother worked in those days. But old habits die hard. I wanted to buy her a refrigerator when we moved to Rose Cottage. Her reaction was, "What do I want a 'fridge for? I've always managed without one".

Appleford was famous then for its home-made wine, particularly cowslip and elderberry. I cannot find mother's recipes for those wines, but I do have her 1920s recipes for rose-hip wine and cherry wine.*

Two of my most vivid memories are of the Second World War. I can still see clearly the day war was declared - a bright, sunny morning - just like any other Sunday. I had just come home from Holy Communion and was skipping in the garden. Father was busy in his vegetable patch digging up potatoes to store for the winter, when mother called from the doorway:

"Billy, Billy, there's a war on".

That Sunday morning many people's lives were about to change dramatically. Mother had been listening to a radio broadcast by the Prime Minister, Mr Neville Chamberlain, announcing in a sombre tone to the British nation that we were at war with Germany.

He said that no dogs and cats were to be on the streets. No lights were to be visible at night. A warm drink and clothing should be available for the children in an air raid shelter and pets would not be admitted.

Father came into the house, put his hand on mother's shoulder and said very quietly and gently:

"Never mind my dear, it will all be over by Christmas".
I believe a lot of people thought that.

I cannot honestly say that our childhood days and early teenage years were spoilt by the war. Visibly the village changed very little. The majority of the younger men were called for military service. Many men, including my father were working on the Great Western Railway when the war started and were exempt

---

*   See recipe at end of book.

from joining the armed forces. Trains had to be kept moving to transport troops and ammunition to the Channel ports, ready to cross to France...and war. Then there were the ambulance trains bringing the wounded soldiers home. I remember waving to the trains – camouflaged in green and brown, with Red Crosses painted on the sides of the carriages. The trains travelled so slowly through the village.

Men, like my father, were expected to help on the farm when they were not on duty on the railway. This workforce was particularly needed at harvest time. For us children the harvest field was another playground. Men and women helped with the stooking - lifting the heavy sheaves of corn and forming them into a wigwam, to dry the corn. This was heavy work. There was always a sheaf of corn saved for the Harvest Festival Service. The boys would go beating for rabbits. Mother made a lovely rabbit pie. Her recipe is at the end of this book.

We would go with our mothers to the harvest field to take a picnic with flasks of tea for us and flagons of home-made wine for the men. The men would have been working since 5 am, gathering in the harvest. As there were no modern combine harvesters in those days, a reaper-binder drawn by two cart horses and led by Mr Chamberlain, the carter, was used to cut the corn, before it was loaded on to the threshing machine.

Of course, we experienced food rationing and sweet rationing. Sweets were exchanged at The Black Horse on a Sunday morning for ration coupons. The other restrictions my parents had to contend with were clothing coupons and the black-out. When we were eleven and went to to Didcot to school, we had to cycle carrying our gas masks.

In many ways life carried on as usual. The baker called every day. The butcher came from Didcot twice a week. Groceries were delivered by the Co-op from Long Wittenham or Walkers Stores from Abingdon. You could buy a two pound jar of apricot jam for 1s.1d and a pound jar of marmalade was 1s.1½d. A packet of Mitre margarine cost 5d. At Christmas-time you could order your wine from Walker's stores. A bottle of port wine cost 2s.9d, sherry was 3s.6d or 4s.6d and ginger wine 1s.11d. May's, the oilman, came from Abingdon every week to sell paraffin for our oil lamps and methylated spirits for the primus stoves. There was always the village shop, owned by Mr and Mrs Jackson, where you could buy anything from a reel of cotton to a railway ticket.

Mrs Stunell and mother started a Welcome Home Fund for the men in the Services. They and other ladies in the village organised whist drives which were held in The Black Horse public house; plays and concerts took place in the big schoolroom. We used to rehearse in Old Thatch. Mother loved playing the piano. Many winter evenings were spent sitting by the fire knitting for men in the Services. Mother, sitting in the lamplight, knitted long sea-boot stockings in thick oiled wool, thick mittens and balaclava helmets. Evacuees came to the village early in the war. We had a brother and sister to stay with us, but they were only in the village a very short time. Their mother came and took them back to London. The only evacuees that stayed for the duration of the war were Sam and Joyce Bell, who lived with Mrs Powell in the cottages near the church. Sam stayed on, married a local girl and now lives in Abingdon.

It was not really until May 1944 that the reality of war came to our village. As we were cycling home from school at about 4 pm there were soldiers all along the Didcot road. They were hiding in the ditches and behind trees. The soldiers were wearing camouflage uniform and had leaves and grass in their hats. They waved and chatted to us children as we cycled home to Appleford. When I arrived at Old Thatch that day there were several soldiers having cups of tea and cakes in our living room. Mother said, "Put your bike away quickly and have a look on the roof". There was a wheelbarrow lying on the thatched roof and my mother said the garden had been littered with orange parachutes, all over father's plants. Apparently the bright orange parachutes were used for transporting guns, spades, wheelbarrows etc. The pure silk white parachutes carried the soldiers safely to earth. Mother went on to say, "I wish you could have seen it, the sky was full of men jumping out of aeroplanes, they looked like giant snowdrops floating down. I have never seen such a sight". Mrs Stunell was down at the farm with her little girl also called Adeline when she heard a shout, "Look out, missus", and a soldier landed right close to her. I only learned in 1994 that three of those young men were drowned in the Thames, near the railway bridge. Black Bridge we always called it. Many of the soldiers gave their parachutes to the ladies of the village in exchange for tea and cakes. These were later returned to the army. I understand the ladies were frightened that they may be in serious trouble if they kept the parachutes. It must have been very tempting; they were made of pure white silk and clothes rationing did not allow for luxury dresses or silk underwear. However, one lady was prosecuted for having military property. She was found guilty in Abingdon Court of 'receiving a parachute from a soldier' and was fined £2. It was exciting for us to see all the soldiers in the village the next day. They had camped in the fields of Manor Farm overnight. The parachute drop was an incident those of us that experienced it will never forget. Little Appleford helped the war effort! It was in June of that year we heard on the radio that a Second Front had been launched and that many men had landed on the beaches of Northern France.

A glimpse into the past would not be complete without a picture of the lives we led in the 1930s and 1940s. Sunday was the Sabbath day – a day of rest. Every Sunday in the morning we would go to Morning Service and in the afternoons walk across the fields to Long Wittenham. In the evening my grandfather would escort grandmother to church, ring the big bell and return to Old Thatch. While the Service was taking place, he would discuss politics with my father. We were not allowed to do any washing, any knitting or needlework on a Sunday, or go out to play.

We were lucky to have a week's holiday every year. Railway workers were entitled to a free privilege ticket which enabled us to go to the seaside for our annual holiday. This privilege ticket also allowed us a monthly trip to Oxford to go shopping. For the sum of 1s.3d return we could catch a train from Appleford Halt to Oxford, calling at Culham and Radley, a journey then of about half-an-hour. We always went to Woolworths for a bag of broken biscuits and a pound of small real beef sausages. Those little sausages, sizzling hot with bread and butter, were a treat for Saturday only. Then we would sort through the broken biscuits for the chocolate bits to eat first.

Very occasionally we would all cycle to Abingdon to the cinema. We would probably see Shirley Temple, George Formby or the skating star, Sonya Henie. It was quite safe to cycle and leave your bikes unlocked.

Winter evenings were spent in the warm living room. We would play ludo, snakes and ladders, card games, snap, happy families and whist. Father taught me draughts and dominoes.

Visits to the theatre were rare. We always went to the New Theatre in Oxford on Boxing Day to the pantomime. There was an annual visit to the London Palladium where father could see the acrobats on the high wire - which was a favourite of his.

On summer evenings, both boys and girls played together with whips and tops, bowling hoops, roller skating, climbing Knapp Tree and sitting in the tree chatting or going to the river to swim and play in the meadow. Sometimes we played football in Mr Pullen's small field called the Grove.

We lived a very simple life in contrast to the life young people live in the 1990s. But without any doubt I had a happy, safe childhood. We could cycle anywhere, roam across the fields, swim in the river, come home in the dark without any fear of being molested or attacked. I pray for my very young grandchildren that life will return to those Victorian standards when it will again be safe to roam the meadows and pick wild flowers or cycle home in the dark. And that the church door will always be unlocked as it was in those days.

The Church of
St Peter and St Paul

*The church itself, dedicated to St Peter and St
Paul, was doubtless founded in the Saxon period
by St Birinus or one of his missionary priests
from Dorchester. No traces of the Saxon church
remain. A new church was built in the twelfth
century, and portions of this Norman church may
still be seen - the round headed arches in the
south entrance, the heavy stone font, the piscina
in the chancel and the springers in the chancel
arch.*

Chapelry of St Peter and St Paul, Appleford
Rev.G.R.Dunstan, 1950

The church standing at the end of Church Street, like Old Thatch,
has a commanding view of Sinodun Hills. On the eastern side
and to the north it faces the Thames and Oxfordshire. There are
two Norman doorways, one sheltered by the porch and another on
the north side which has been filled up. The font is about the
same period. The priest's doorway and a lancet window belong to
the thirteenth century:

*The church of Appleford belonged to Abingdon
Abbey in 1291 but became subsequently a chapel
of ease to Sutton Courtenay. The chapel yard
was made a burial place in 1749.*

Victoria County History of Berkshire,
1924 edition

In these early days the church and the humble people of this tiny
hamlet were controlled by the influential and powerful Benedictine
monks, who lived in the Abbey in Abingdon. In 1551 when the
manor of Appleford was given to Sir John Mason, his family and

the Justice family, were the most influential and important ones in the village. There are still monuments to both families in the church. The large tombs in the churchyard, enclosed by ornate iron railings under the east wall of the church are those of Walter and Eliza and Thomas and Martha Justice.

There are no longer any members of either the Justice or Mason family living in the village. But their interest in the parish received substantial proof in 1885-6, when renovations were carried out to the church at the expense of Walter Justice. He added the tower, spire and porch; he also gave a stained glass window to be placed at the east end. The design for these alterations were made by Sir Gilbert Scott (1811-1878), an English architect who led the English Gothic revival. He was also associated with the restoration of Westminster Abbey.

> *In addition to a new roof, it involved a new porch and vestry, the lengthening of the nave by five feet six inches, the rebuilding of the nave walls and the chancel arch, and the renewal of all internal fittings except the font. The Ecclesiastical Commissioners for England restored the chancel at the same time. The tower was equipped for a ring of six bells. Three new ones were cast by John Warner and Sons of Cripplegate, London, who also re-cast the former treble bell which had been made at Witney in 1710. These were then added to the two older bells which were cast in the fourteenth century at the great medieval foundry at Wokingham.*
>
> From a leaflet produced for the Patronal Festival, St.Peter's Day 1986 to mark the centenary of the Renovations.

I know my grandfather was a bell ringer, so too was Joe Brown of School House.

Mention should be made of the small organ built in 1777 which originally belonged to the Abbey House at Sutton Courtenay and is one of the very few organs made by Samuel Green to have survived.

In the 1930s the church always had a good congregation when the Rev.Hugh Scanlon was vicar. There was always a full choir. Mr William Powell, who lived in the farm cottages near the church was the choir master and Mr Frederick Clifton of No. 2 Rose Cottages, the tenor. There were always several boys from school in the choir. I understand there are only three choristers now.

In former days it was the custom for the villagers to beat the bounds of the parish on Ascension Day. This fact comes to light through the 'Presentments to the Archdeacon of Berkshire by the churchwardens', originally preserved in the Bodleian Library, from which we learn that:

> On 7th June 1673, John Whichelowe and Katherine Whichelowe, widow, failed in their duty which was to 'provide two bushells of malte to be brued in beare, against Ascension Day' for the inhabitants of the village when they go the perambulation. The wheat and malt were given 'to be yeat and drunken by John Whichelowe the Elder', lately deceased in or against his new barne, according to his true will and meaning.
> We have no idea how John and Katherine were brought to a sense of this obligation, but from the same source it appears that they repented their default in 'not making an eatinge and drinkinge on Ascension Day', for on 15th June the following year the parson says crisply, 'They have provided it now'.

One of my grandfather's stories was of the church ghost, which nobody had ever seen. It was said to be buried beneath an altar-tomb, in the churchyard. The ghost disliked village schoolboys sharpening their pocket knives upon his final home and sneaked out to remove the offending schoolboy knives!

Mrs Dorothy Bell, a teacher, who lived in one of the bungalows in Main Road remembers the vicar visiting her on his bicycle in 1938. She said there were more church services then both morning, afternoon and evening every Sunday. There were large congregations and she was deeply disturbed that the number of services had been cut and congregations had deteriorated during her years in the village.

It was in 1973 or 1974 that the silver cross was stolen from the altar by a drunken man. He went to the river, threw it in and fell asleep on the river bank. When he awoke he remembered what he had done, went to the police and confessed. The vicar at the time was the Rev. George Jaegar who forgave the thief. The silver cross was replaced by a brass one which was given to the church by Mr Currie, who was the organist at the time, and it is still on the altar today.

Two other graves must be included here. The unmarked grave of John Faulkner, the aforementioned jockey. Mrs Stunell remembered his funeral and knew where the grave was. Sadly, she died in December 1995 before she had been able to show me where it is in the churchyard. She did tell me that John Faulkner died in February 1933 just before his 105th birthday. His coffin was taken from his home in Main Road to the church in one of Farmer Pullen's wagons. The wagon was pulled by one of his heavy carthorses. Picture in your mind, a cold February day and a horse with shining brasses pulling an old wagon, laden with flowers and the coffin. The majority of the mourners followed on foot, wearing their Sunday best caps and long overcoats, all with black armbands. It was then traditional to wear a black armband for some six weeks after a bereavement. On the day of the funeral curtains would be drawn in all the houses, as a mark of respect to the dead.

The other grave and headstone I include here is that of 2620462 Grenadier Sidney G. Broughton. He was the only serviceman from the village to be killed in the Second World War. A Grenadier Guard, he was killed when the Guards Chapel in

London was bombed by a German flying bomb on June 18th 1944. These bombs were fired from Northern France and Belgium without a pilot but with sufficient fuel to reach London. When the fuel ran out the bomb fell to earth. The chapel was filled with Guardsmen attending a morning service when the bomb dropped. Before he joined the army Sidney Broughton was a ploughman at Manor Farm and lived with his mother and brother Arthur in one of the cottages that stood almost opposite Rose Cottages – next door to the Faulkner family.

Manor Farm

Richard Turpin, the notorious highwayman, made the Manor Farm his headquarters when 'working' the London-Oxford road, the ford offering facilities if pursuit recommended transfer of himself and his booty from the Berkshire to the Oxfordshire side of the river. The oak table at which the man ate his meals, long in possession of the Pullen family whose representative still holds the farm, was an object of interest until sold for 100 guineas.

The Berkshire Book

The village in the seventeenth century was strongly Puritan. When Royalist cavalry under Prince Rupert came, there was sharp fighting in the vicinity; the Royalists set fire to many of the houses, but so vigorously were they attacked by the village people that they retreated, pursued as far as Oxford by the men of Appleford, a long way when the men were on foot. The Ordnance Survey map, surveyed 1872-5, and revised in 1932, carries the words 'human remains, discovered 1890', which could indicate a find of archaeological interest comparable with the urns and skeletons of Saxon time unearthed during the construction of the railway line in 1842.

Although the village school was available for all the children, many parents employed on the land were reluctant to have their children educated. They did not consider it necessary. A ploughman did not need an education! It was far better for them to be employed on the farm and bring a few shillings into the home.

In The Berkshire Book we learn of a case of child labour which shows what work was expected of small boys early in the eighteenth century. The two young sons of Paul Orpwood, who died in 1716, were aged twelve and fourteen when employed by Richard Truelock 'in going to plow, looking after horses and other ordinary work'. They were then working for themselves to provide their own clothes. Truelock paid the boys respectively 2s and 1s.6d per week and paid John Nevill of Appleford £5 a year for their keep.

Manor Farm, lying west of the church, is an ancient building and probably represents the grange of Abingdon Abbey. In 1551 the King granted the manor of Appleford, and the advowson of the chapel to Sir John Mason. He and his wife, Elizabeth, made a settlement in 1558 and when Sir John died in 1566 the manor of Appleford passed to Anthony Weekes, who took the name of Mason.

On the death of Elizabeth in 1589 Manor Farm passed to Thomas Reade of Barton House Abingdon and his heirs. Thomas Reade died in December 1604 and his son, John, died childless in the following January. The heir to the property became John's elder brother, Sir Thomas Reade.

Manor Farm descended to Sir Thomas Reade with Barton House and remained in that family until Sir John Chandon Reade sold it in about 1820.

The new owner was Charles Eyston of Hendred, whose grandson John Joseph Eyston was the owner in 1924.

It would have been early in Charles Eyston's ownership of the farm that the agricultural depression had a devastating effect on the men working on the land. Farmers were forced to cut costs and one of the first cuts was in labour, either by cutting the men's wages or laying them off work. The situation in the whole area around Appleford was so bad that there were riots for a week in 1830. But an attempt by men from neighbouring parishes to create a riot in Appleford failed.

Wages for an adult working on the farm did not improve a great deal. In the nineteenth century the agricultural wages paid in Berkshire were amongst the lowest in England. In the 1830s the wage was about 7s a week, and by the beginning of the First

World War the average wage for a man working on the land was 12s.6d a week. Not a lot with which to raise a family – often a large one. Although the man was given a cottage to live in, with free milk and vegetables, he was still poorly paid when compared to a Great Western Railwayman, who was earning nearly £2 a week.

When I lived in Old Thatch in the early 1930s, the tenant farmer was Mr Henry 'Harry' Pullen. Manor Farm and most of the property in Church Street then belonged to Squire Eyston of East Hendred. Mr Pullen was known in the village as a gentleman farmer, very respected by the village people. He lived in the farmhouse with his wife and four daughters. I am told when 'Old Harry Pullen was farmer no villager was ever short of vegetables, although he preferred to be asked for produce and not have it stolen from his land'. Such was his generosity when asked to finance a football pitch on the recreation ground, he replied, 'Well, I suppose I should, but I expect you will still use my Grove'. The footballers got their new pitch. He was right, as we were still playing football in the Grove when I was at school. Mr Pullen's daughter, Helen, started a Scout troop for the village boys. One of the farm outhouses was used for meetings.

This was the day of the horse drawn plough. Mr Ernest Chamberlain was the carter. Carters were very proud of their horses and particularly their appearance. The horses wore full sets of highly polished brasses and often had their manes and tails braided with ribbons and straw. Some of these brasses were very old and passed down from father to son. I have one of these old brasses and a small brass bell, given to me by my grandfather. A memento of the days when he worked on the farm in the Second World War.

During that war the Coalition Government announced a period of double summer time, when we altered the clocks in the spring by two hours instead of the customary one. This was for the benefit of the farmers, to help them during the hay-making season and to gather the harvest in. I remember those long sunny summer evenings when we swam in the river and as we all grew older, helped in the harvest field.

Three ploughman were employed at the beginning of the war, George Meadham, Sidney Broughton and Frank Holman. The tractor driver was George Collett. There was a milkman in charge of the dairy herd. We were able to walk to the farm and buy a can of warm milk, straight from the cow's udder every morning. Milk was poured into large milk churns and collected by lorry from the farm gate every day. There were also men employed as general labourers. They helped to look after the sheep that usually grazed in the field adjoining the churchyard. There used to be a sheep dip just inside the gate. At harvest time a threshing machine was hired from Charlie Alder of Crowmarsh.

When Mr Pullen died in January 1939, his death was reported in the North Berks Herald on January 20th, 1939:

> *The death of Mr Harry Pullen, aged 71, on Tuesday at Manor Farm, Appleford, removed from the district a member of a well known farming family. After being in business in London, he farmed in Dorchester for nearly 10 years and, on the death of his father, some 20 years ago, took over Manor Farm, Appleford. He was a member of Abingdon Board of Guardians and for some years a member of the Abingdon R.D.C., retiring about five years ago.*
>
> *The following employees acted as bearers at his funeral: Chamberlain, Wyatt, Barnett, Woodley, Lacey and Prior.*

The farm was then worked for a short time by a Mr Bill Diamond who retired to live in Orchard House. Then the farm passed into the hands of Mr Edward Gale, who with his wife and three children lived there for some years. Manor Farm is now worked by his eldest son, Patrick.

When Harry Pullen's widow moved to Oxford to live with one of her daughters, the contents of the house, including the oak table

Dick Turpin is said to have used, were auctioned in the farmyard. I can just remember that day. My father bought a small chair, which was part of a suite. This suite consisted of a settee, two large armchairs and four smaller chairs, for Mr Pullen's daughters. These were sold separately. I still have my chair - made of rosewood, inlaid with mother-of-pearl - which cost my father £1.10s.

Barnards

Barnards was possibly the home of a yeoman, the original part of the house was built in the seventeenth century (not before 1632) consisted of 3 rooms up and 3 down, with seventeenth century beams. Two and a half centuries later, round about 1890, a kitchen, hall, W.C, 2 bedrooms and one bathroom were added. Around 1900 the dining room, a new entrance hall and front stairs were added. Also the master bedroom, bathroom W.C and dressing room. In 1920s or 30s a kitchen, dining room, W.C, with a further sitting room and bedroom. Bay windows were added at the same time.

From plans of the house in the possession of
Major Robertson

Barnards is one of the largest house in the village, the original part of the property dating back to Charles II, with later additions either side. It is similar to another house which belonged to a yeoman, Orchard House. It stands at the end of a long drive and in my childhood the large iron gates at the entrance were always closed and locked. In early spring the right hand side of the drive was covered with yellow aconites – they were so lovely to see after the dark days of winter. The grounds of the house at the rear extended from a terraced garden to an orchard and a field which reached the river bank. There was a small boat house on the river which belonged to the house. To the east of the house there was an area of lawn, with a path which led to the family chapel and then to the school.

In my memory Barnards was an important house in the village. During my childhood it was owned by the Stuart-Menteath family. Other owners, according to Kelly's Directory of the

1920s, were: 1920 Miss Heberden, 1924 Mrs Dearden and in 1931 Mrs Tallboys

It had been suggested to me that an MP, Frank Gray, lived in Barnards in the 1920s. However, the Rt. Hon John Patten MP wrote to me in July 1994:

> '...it is possible that the MP in question could have been a tenant rather than the owner – Major Ralph Glyn was member for Berkshire in 1924 but according to Who's Who he lived in Wantage.'

Frank Gray was MP for Oxford City 1922–1924 and it is possible he also rented the property for a time.

In the 1930s, when Mrs Tallboys lived there, the annual Flower Show was held in the grounds. The field and tennis courts, which were used for the Show, are now private houses and gardens. It was preceded by a procession of horses from the farm, with their brasses shining brightly. Appleford was famous for its gardeners. Mr John Wedlake of 'Gwalia', Church Street was one of the prime movers in the formation of the Appleford Horticultural Society and for several years was the honorary secretary. He died in 1939 aged seventy-two. All the allotments were worked and every cottage had a fine vegetable garden. Competition at the Flower Show was very fierce in the village and there was always a good display. There were classes for children and a favourite one was a jam jar of wild flowers. The school children were taken to Long Meadow to gather their flowers. There was also a Children's Fancy Dress Competition. The day was completed by a Flannel Dance held in the house and grounds, so called because grey flannels were fashionable men's trousers at the time.

Mr and Mrs Menteath and their two sons were the next family to live in Barnards. They arrived in the village in the 1930s and remained during the war years. It is not surprising that they were a popular family in the village. Mrs Menteath did a great deal of good work for the village people, including being a school governor. I have mentioned earlier the caring and progressive work she did for the school. She also started a Women's Institute and later became its President. The W.I. meetings were held in the school. It was reported in the North Berkshire Herald in April 1939 that:

> *Patchwork was the subject of a demonstration at the monthly meeting given by Miss Walthau, who also exhibited some fine quilting. Mrs Stuart-Menteath (president) presided, supported by Miss Tolson and Miss Jenkins. The competition (six household hints cut from a newspaper) being judged by Mrs Bradbrooke. Games and dancing followed to music by Mrs Lacey at the piano.*

Mrs Menteath was responsible for starting First Aid classes which took place in Barnards. She allowed the fifteenth century chapel to be used for wedding receptions, birthday parties, cricket club teas and whist drives. When the parachute landing took place in the village, three young parachutists drowned in the River Thames and were laid to rest there.

Whenever there was a special event such as a Coronation or Jubilee or a feast day, the village school children were invited to Barnards for tea. We took the maypole and danced on the lawn, weaving intricate patterns with the gaily coloured ribbons. Country dancing classes and Sports Days were held there on the lawn. The children were always given a present.

In the evenings after special occasions there would be a dance, the house and grounds were decorated with fairy lights, and a dance band was engaged for the evening. Many of the ladies of the village were employed on these occasions. I remember my mother telling me of the happy parties that were held at there. The Stuart-Menteath family sold the house after the war and moved away from the village.

Over the years the house has lost a great deal of its land. The field, orchard and most of the long garden have gone.

The Post Office

Thinking of the transport problem, I look back with yearning to the many trains which stopped at the Halt, which was built in 1933. One could, without the aid of a timetable, stroll down to the Halt and be sure of a train to Oxford or Didcot. Tickets for the trains were obtainable from the Post Office.
Memoirs of Dorothy Bell, School Teacher at Appleford and Long Wittenham

The Shop, Jacksons, the Post Office – whatever we called it – the tiny village shop was an integral part of village life. The building, now Post Office Cottage, stands on the corner of Church Street. In the early 1920s it was owned by Mr and Mrs Berry. Mrs Berry was the postwoman and walked all the village and up to Pearith Farm to deliver mail and empty the Pearith letter box. It must have been a long walk on a wet, cold morning. When Mr and Mrs Berry retired in 1926, the village marked the occasion with a social and whist drive which was held in the schoolroom. During the evening a presentation was made to the retiring postmaster and his wife. It was reported in the North Berks Herald that the collection was made in the village by Mrs Jennings and appreciation was shown by all present at the evening for the services rendered by Mr and Mrs Berry.

The couple made their new home in one of the terraced cottages, called the Six-Row. This row of cottages stood in Main Road, backing on to the allotments. The water to all these homes was supplied by one well.

In the late 1920s Mr and Mrs Jackson bought the Post Office and village shop. Mrs Jackson had been a Court dress-maker and her husband, an ex-soldier, suffered from gas poisoning caused when he was fighting in the trenches in France in the First World

War. Mrs Jackson was the post mistress and was employed by the Great Western Railway to sell railway tickets. Mr Jackson occasionally served in the shop and they had one son called Billy.

When you opened the shop door, a bell would tinkle to let Mrs Jackson know you were there. As you opened the door you faced the Post Office counter. In the left hand corner were the railway tickets and a machine to punch the date on the tickets when they were sold. In the middle of the shop was a long glass counter, which contained a variety of goods – postcards of the village, birthday cards, cottons and bars of chocolate. The shelves behind were stacked with groceries. You could buy butter, cereals, dried fruit, cheese, soap, toilet rolls and biscuits. Indeed, if you handed an order to Mrs Jackson in the morning it would be ready to be picked up in the evening. I remember going every Saturday for a bar of Cadburys chocolate costing 2d. My father would buy a packet of Woodbine cigarettes for 1s.0d. Mrs Jackson sold a variety of cigarettes – Players, Kensitas, Ardath, Woodbines, Players Weights, Gold Flake and Passing Cloud for Mrs Clifford. We would also have the accumulator charged. Accumulators were like batteries that gave power to the wireless sets possessed by some of the village people.

Selling railway tickets was a large part of Mrs Jackson's business. You could buy a ticket to almost anywhere in the country. In the 1930s the return fare to Oxford was 1s.0d – after 4 pm it was 9d; the return fare to Didcot was 6d and on market days 4½d. Occasionally, when there was a football match in Reading, one could buy a special football ticket for 1s.11d, provided you caught the 1.18 pm train.

I remember running with my friends to the shop to buy a 6d return ticket to Didcot. We would catch the 5.20 pm train and go to the cinema on a Saturday evening. A cinema seat cost 1s.6d. We could buy a 6d bag of chips on the way home and be in time for the 9.20 pm train back, to Appleford. After the last train had gone, the gas lights would be extinguished.

In 1935 Mrs Grace Fidler was appointed Appleford's postwoman. She was supplied with a navy blue uniform, jacket, skirt and cap and a Post Office bicycle. Mrs Fidler's day started early when she met the 7.29 am train. Having collected the mail, she would take it to the Post Office to be sorted. Her round would start in Church Street, followed by School Lane before cycling over the railway bridge to Bridge House and Bridge Farm; then up Main Road, across the railway level-crossing to Radcott Farm, continuing on to Hill Farm and the three cottages. Her round finished at Pearith Farm, where she emptied the post box near the Didcot Road junction and returned to the Post Office. Having tied up the outgoing mail she put it on the 11 am train to Oxford. The village postwoman's day was over. Mrs Fidler delivered our mail every day, whatever the weather and always with a cheery smile. She retired in 1969 and her daughter Iris took the job over until 1972. Letters are now delivered by vans from Abingdon.

Mrs Jackson retired when Mr Jackson died. The Post Office and village store opened in the bungalow in Main Road. This had been built when the cottages opposite Rose Cottages were demolished. Mrs Paul became the post mistress but sadly, the Post Office closed a few years ago and now there is no longer a village shop.

The Village Pubs

*THIS INDENTURE   made the sixth day of August one thousand, eight hundred and ninety one...
BETWEEN Daniel Robert Featon Esquire the Secretary for the time being of the Board of Charity Commissioners for England and Wales and as such 'The Official Trustee of Charity Lands' hereinafter called the Official Trustee of the first part The Reverend Richard John Howard Rice of Sutton Courtenay in the County of Berks Clerk in Holy Orders. William Pullen of Sutton Courtenay.... Edward Pullen of Appleford.... Charles Tame of Appleford... being the Trustees of Edmund Bradstock's Charity for the poor of the hamlet of Appleford of the second part and Thomas Townsend and John Matthew Townsend being Co-partners in the trade or business of Brewers at Abingdon... of the third part...*

Assignment of
a long Leasehold Public House
Orchard Land and Garden situate at
Appleford in the County of Berks
6th August 1891

This is the first evidence I have been able to find of the existence of The Carpenters Arms in the village. It clearly shows that this land and buildings were a part of the Edmund Bradstock Charity. The Indenture goes on to say that the Trustees of the Charity were authorised to '*sell all the estate and interest of the Charity in the land and premises...for not less than six hundred and fifty pounds...all that public house (known as The Carpenters Arms)...with the outbuildings yard garden land orchard and*

paddock...now occupied by Henry Bullock as under tenant to be
sold to Thomas Townsend and John Matthew Townsend.'

There is no information to say why the name The Carpenters
Arms was used, but it would be fairly safe to assume there was a
carpenters' workshop there at some time.

My grandfather thought the public house was built on the site of
an old coaching inn. Certainly the forge used to be there before
Mr Jennings, the blacksmith, transferred the business to his home
in Main Road, near the signalbox. I remember the Green which
was in front of the inn with wooden railings along the roadside.

Both The Carpenters Arms and The Black Horse, which used to
stand almost opposite one another in Main Road, were Morland
public houses. I feel a little should be told of the origin of
Morland of Abingdon.

> *In 1711 John Morland, a farmer, purchased a*
> *property in the village of West Ilsey some twelve*
> *miles south of Abingdon. The original deed is in*
> *the Berkshire Records Office and describes the*
> *vendor as Benjamin Smith, a maltster. Soon after*
> *acquiring the maltings John and his son*
> *Benjamin ventured into brewing and traces of*
> *their brewhouses can be seen today.*

from Morland plc
The Brewery, Ock Street, Abingdon

Morland moved their brewery business in the early 1900s to The
Vineyard, Abingdon. The thriving business is now firmly
established in Ock Street.

I remember the Green in front of The Carpenters Arms being
used for the annual Appleford Feast. It was held on St Peter's
Day, the 29th June, unless that day fell on a Sunday. There were
swing-boats, roundabouts, chair-o-planes and many side shows.
The travelling fair was always popular in the village. I understand
in earlier days a horse fair was held here, bringing business for
the pub and the blacksmith. The Green is now a tarmacadam car
park.

Until 1959 when it was demolished, The Black Horse pub stood a few feet back from the Main Road. When I was at school the landlord of this pub was Mr 'Dick' Harvey who lived there with his wife and their three children, Douglas, Peter and Jean. I have no idea how old this building was, but there was a little cottage attached to it, which Mr John Meadham tells me used to be the village bakehouse where residents could take their Sunday dinners for roasting.

I knew The Black Horse as the home of my contemporary, Jean Harvey. Jean and I used to cycle to Didcot school together, and after school would play together in the family rooms. The pub had three public rooms, including the bar, where I understand John Faulkner had his special chair in his own corner. Nobody ever sat in it after he entered the bar. He was a well-known raconteur with many tales of the turf. Everybody knew 'Old John'. He had his own horses – Biscuit, which it is said he rode in the Grand National and Rip Van Winkle which, though bought for only five shillings, won several races.

John broke his thigh at the age of ninety, something to do with a mule. His doctor said, "You'll never work again". "We'll see", said Old John. Some seven weeks later he walked to Abingdon and back – a good eight miles. It is said his last words were to ask for a glass of beer. When he was unable to drink it his family knew 'the old man was finished'. He had reached his last hurdle.

The bar which John used was for men only. There was also a large comfortable lounge bar with a piano and a warm fire in the winter months. The public rooms were completed by a very small room - known as the Tap Room. Jean's father was responsible for the formation of the Appleford Home Guard during the Second World War and so the pub was used as its Headquarters.

Mr Harvey allowed the lounge bar to be used for whist drives and always provided refreshments for the players. After the war he organised charabanc outings and drove the vehicle to a seaside resort for the day. It was a very enjoyable occasion and there was always a coach full of happy day trippers bound for Southsea or a similar resort. It was probably the only time many people saw the sea. To the right of the public house there was a very pretty garden, where families could sit and enjoy a drink. In the grounds behind the pub there used to be a row of four cottages. One of these was destroyed by fire, the remainder were demolished and the tenants re-housed in the village. The Black Horse was much used during the war, many soldiers would walk across the fields from Didcot and spend an evening in the village hostelry.

The Carpenters Arms, now the only village pub, has a large car park, a pleasant garden to sit in and a restaurant where you can enjoy a Sunday roast or have a snack at the bar.

Changing Times

It is nearly 50 years since I left Appleford and many old customs and traditions no longer exist.

The village school, built in 1607, was a dream of Appleford's benefactor, Edmund Bradstock. A dream that came true: he wanted all the children of the poor to have a free education for all time. Sadly that aspiration came to an end when the school closed in 1961 and the buildings were reduced to rubble. Large houses and bungalows now stand in School Lane.

The Halt is still there and there is still a very good train service to Oxford in one direction and Didcot, Reading and London Paddington in the other. All the Great Western Railwaymen have gone. In the 1930s men were proud to be Great Western Railwaymen, they had a social standing in the village. You must remember this was still a village with Victorian standards and values. There was most definitely a class system. A railwayman's wage was relatively high and some of these men would have considered themselves to be middle class.

Knapp Tree no longer stands proudly at the centre of the village. This grand old tree and the surrounding green area was another playground for us children in the 1930s and 1940s. Legend had it that if a baby was not born in the village every year, Knapp Tree would fall down. This story was never put to the test. The tree has now been cut down by the local council because it was felt to be unsafe.

Of course, the motor car is now the most usual form of transport in the village. Gone are the days when everyone walked the three-and-a-half miles to Abingdon for a visit to the market each Monday. My grandfather was one of these, and once a year he would walk his pigs to sell them at the cattle market. In earlier days men and boys would go to Oxford to St. Giles Fair on foot, a distance of about ten miles. Luckily for us we lived in the era of the bicycle – as older children we cycled everywhere. For necessity both to school and later to work, and for pleasure, perhaps to the cinema in Abingdon. We would cycle to dances in Sutton Courtenay or Long Wittenham or to Wittenham Clumps for a picnic. The cricket teams cycled to all away matches – carrying bats and pads on the handlebars or carriers of bikes.

The two streets in the village – Main Road and Church Street have been joined by a new housing estate, Chambrai Close. This estate is built on the orchard and land which used to belong to Mr and Mrs Denning, who lived in the house called Kings Weston near Knapp Tree. There are new houses on Barnards' land and School Lane, also in the Grove in Church Street. With the new houses the population has increased considerably. A table in 'A History of Berkshire' shows the population in 1801 to be 200 and in 1901 to be 251. It is now considerably higher than this. The 1991 census shows the population to be 355 – males 186, females 169. Total dwellings 127. Total number of cars 199 – I mention this as a contrast to the Appleford of the 1930s and 1940s when the majority of us had a cycle but very few had cars.

It does seem a great pity that all the little children from the old and new houses have to leave the village to be educated, travelling the three-and-a-half miles to Didcot each day. I wonder at the wisdom of closing an excellent village school.

Progress and new technology has made some improvements to the village. Electricity came after the Second World War. In 1959 mains water was laid to the village, but it was not until 1963 that main drainage reached Appleford, although there are still no street lights in the village.

Some, like me, will remember Penn Copse – a small copse along the Sutton Courtenay road, which was a favourite spot to walk to in early spring to pick wild violets. The ground was always a mass of purple and white with these lovely tiny flowers. Alas, Penn Copse has also gone, having been grubbed out and ploughed.

Remembering this tiny woodland area revives memories of the Traction Engines Rally which used to take place in the adjacent field in the 1950s. It was Arthur Napper of Bridge Farm, who introduced traction engine racing to the village. In doing so he gave pleasure to a large number of people. In the summer of 1950 Mr Napper challenged his friend Mr Miles Chetwynd-Stapyleton to race their engines – the loser to buy the winner a firkin (nine gallons) of beer. This friendly challenge brought fame to the village. One sunny afternoon all the villagers were invited to watch this race between his 1902 Marshall engine, 'Old Timer' and Mr Chetwynd-Stapyleton's 1918 Aveling and Porter engine, 'Lady Grove'. This first race was won by Mr Napper. The day and racing was so exciting it became an annual event for several years.

I do remember getting up early to watch these magnificent old machines, puffing and huffing, trundling along Main Road to the race ground. Their paintwork was always immaculate, their brasswork highly polished and shining brightly. They were a product of the best of British engineering.

After Sunday dinner we would all walk round the road to the races. There were always side-shows, a fun fair, beer tents and refreshments to enjoy.

These old machines were primarily used for threshing and created different jobs for the men working in agriculture. Many men then broke with tradition and learned new skills. The engines needed drivers, fitters and engineers and if they could obtain employment on a weekly basis they would probably be better off than the man still working as a farm labourer.

Along with the passing of the Great Western Railwayman, the skilled farm worker, the carter, the pigman, the ploughman and his horse have all gone from the land. With the coming of the combine harvester the threshing strapper is not required. In 1950 there were 918,000 agricultural workers in the UK. In 1994 this number was reduced to 253,000. Mr Curry, the last local shoemaker and repairer died some years ago. The traditional crafts and skills are no longer needed in this age of technology at the end of the twentieth century.

I am sure there will be stories to tell of this new age in the village. I have not researched the village since it became Appleford, Oxfordshire. Perhaps in future someone will have the pleasure of writing their memories of a new Appleford. I hope so.

Betty Reynolds outside Old Thatch, 1930's.

Appleford Christmas Pudding

½ lb	finely shredded suet
1 lb	eggs weighed in their shells
1 lb	dried plums, stoned and halved
1 lb	mixed peel, cut in long strips
1 lb	small raisins
1 lb	sultanas
1 lb	currants
1 lb	sifted flour
1 lb	sugar
1 lb	brown bread crumbs

1 teaspoon (heaped) mixed spice
Half a nutmeg - grated
2 teaspoons salt
½ pint new milk
juice of one lemon
a very large wineglass brandy

Method

Mix the dry ingredients. Moisten with the eggs, beaten to a froth, add the milk, lemon juice and brandy mixed. Stand for at least twelve hours in a cool place, then turn into buttered basins. Boil for eight hours at first, then for two hours before serving.

This quantity makes three puddings of about three pounds each.

Betty Reynolds'
Wine Recipes

Rose Hip Wine

3½ lb   Rose hips
3½ lb   sugar
1 gallon of boiling water

Wash the hips - cut in half. Put them in a bowl. Pour on boiling water. Stir well. Cover and leave for two weeks. Strain, add the sugar, stir well until dissolved. Cover and leave for five days. Bottle and store in a <u>dark</u> place.

The wine was left to brew in large earthenware bowls, bottled and kept in a dark cupboard to be ready for Christmas.

Cherry Wine

5 lb   Black Cherries
3½ lb   sugar
1 gallon cold water
¼ oz   yeast

Place cherries in saucepan - crush with wooden spoon. Pour on one gallon of cold water, bring to boil. Simmer until cherries are tender. Remove from heat. Strain liquid off. Then tip cherries into a muslin bag and squeeze gently to get remaining juice out. Add the sugar and the yeast. Stir well. Cover bowl and leave for three days, stirring well daily. Then bottle, leave cork loose until fermenting is complete. Then cork tight.

Mrs Reynolds' Rabbit Pie

1 rabbit
½ lb of bacon or pickled pork
½ lb of beef steak
½ pint of stock
salt and pepper
short crust or puff-pastry

Method

Wash the rabbit, divide it into small joints, cut the beef into small thin slices, and the pork into dice. Place these ingredients in layers, in a pie dish. Season each layer liberally with salt and pepper, cover with pastry. Bake from $1^3/_4$ to 2 hours in a brisk oven until the pastry has risen and set, and afterwards more slowly. Before serving, add the remainder of the hot stock to the pie. When the pie is intended to be eaten cold, force meat balls and hard boiled eggs will be found an improvement, and the appearance may be improved by brushing over with yolk of egg when three-parts baked.

Time: To bake, from $1^3/_4$ to 2 hours
Sufficient for 6 persons